The Basis of Early Christian Theism

Lawrence Thomas Cole

Contents

CHAPTER I INTRODUCTION 7
CHAPTER II GREEK AND ROMAN THEISTIC ARGUMENTS 10
CHAPTER III THE PATRISTIC POINT OF VIEW 20
CHAPTER IV PATRISTIC USE OF THE THEISTIC ARGUMENTS 30
CHAPTER V ECLECTIC THEISM 44

THE BASIS OF EARLY CHRISTIAN THEISM

BY

Lawrence Thomas Cole

CHAPTER I
INTRODUCTION

A question which every author ought to ask of himself before he sends forth his work, and one which must occur to every thoughtful reader, is the inquiry, **Cui bono?**--what justification has one for treating the subject at all, and why in the particular way which he has chosen? To the pertinency of this question to the present treatise the author has been deeply sensible, and therefore cannot forbear a few prefatory words of explanation of his object and method.

In accounts of the theistic argument, as in the history of philosophy in general, it has been customary to pass over a space of well-nigh ten centuries of the Christian era in silence, or with such scanty and unsympathetic notice as to make silence the better alternative. Largely through the influence of such treatment as this, we moderns have almost forgotten at times that during this period there lived men inferior to none in history in endowments of mind and influence on succeeding generations, and that there then took place some of the most significant and far-reaching intellectual conflicts in the history of thought. "With Cicero," says Professor Stirling, "we reached in our course a most important and critical halting place.... We have still ... to wait those thousand years yet before Anselm shall arrive with what is to be named the new proof, the proof ontological, and during the entire interval it is the Fathers of the Church and their immediate followers who, in repetition of the old, or suggestion of the new, connect thinker with thinker, philosopher with philosopher, pagan with Christian."[1] To attempt to account for even one of the details of thought during this period cannot be without its advantages.

For Christianity gave a new and unique turn to thought. It brought with it a new set of data, and a new subject-matter. The Christian doctrine of God, the distinctions in the Trinity, the great doctrines centering around the person of Jesus

Christ, though, perhaps, faintly foreshadowed in some of the earlier speculations, are, in their fulness and completeness, first given to the world by the Founder of Christianity. The claims made for these doctrines, too, gave them a unique character. In contrast with the half-hearted, faltering conclusions of the prevalent philosophical schools, Christianity asserted that its teachings were absolute truth; it claimed to be nothing less than a revelation from the Creator of the world. It will be readily seen that the introduction of such a system as this into the Greek world would be attended with important results, not only in its effects upon the intellectual life of the times, but also in the influence of the current philosophical conceptions on the statement of its doctrine. The significance of this early period lies in the fact that, in the positive, definite system of Christianity, systematic thought, which was fast becoming disorganized and sceptical, found a center about which it might rally and focus itself, and the scattered fragments of philosophy were all collected together, by either friends or foes, about the new religion. The new point of view and the new relations would be most significant, too, in that department of thought with which the contact of this new central system had most to do, and thus the treatment of the theistic problem exhibits in a special degree the alteration in the standpoint and method of philosophy. It threw into bold relief the old basis of belief in the divine, and aroused a comparison and discussion of the validity of the various arguments hitherto used by speculative thought, and set them over in sharp contrast to the claims of the new revelation. In the early period when this contrast was most clearly felt, and time had not yet permitted a complete fusion and blending of the two points of view, we find a simplicity of situation which will aid analysis and facilitate the study of the relation of the old arguments for the existence of a God to the Christian doctrine, and which will help in determining the elements due to each and in interpreting the reasons for the direction of thought on this subject, which characterized the whole of the Mediaeval period.

In the representations of early Christian thought, however, we find great differences in the emphasis laid upon the speculative side of the theistic problem. Christian philosophy is no exception to the rule that the thought of the race develops through the needs, temperaments and tendencies with which it comes into contact, and unfolds itself naturally in response to internal or external stimuli--the doubts, intellectual needs and growing consciousness and experience of the believer, and the cavils, objections and attacks of his opponent. The first Christian teachers had to meet simple problems, and the mission of the Apostolic and sub-Apostolic Church was to "the people." Its first task, determined by the conditions in which the Christians found themselves, as well as by the command of their Master, was to convert the Jews, who, by their long training as a "peculiar people," were especially adapted for receiving this new revelation, based, as it was, on that monotheistic idea to the preservation of which their national life had been devoted. Upon them the primitive Christians, most of whom, like St. Paul, were "Hebrews of the Hebrews," brought to bear the instrument most adapted to their conversion, namely, the argument deduced from the sacred Scriptures of their race.

And when the Church finally turned towards the Gentile world, it was still the popular religion, the religion of the poets, rather than the philosophy of the schools, with which its apologists first came into contact, and it is very evident from such writings as the recently recovered ***Apology*** of Aristides, "philosopher of Athens," and many other works extending over the whole Ante-Nicene period, that much of the energy of the early exponents of Christianity was directed towards the conversion of the populace who still adhered, at least formally, to the religion of their own poets.

The function of the primitive Christians, so far as the content of their belief was concerned, was to preserve and transmit to their successors an ***implicit*** faith. The value of this faith they attempted to show chiefly by practical, ethical demonstration. Thus they preached chiefly by example, and it is on the ground of ***life*** rather than that of ***thought*** that they made their plea to the Gentiles. In their struggle for existence, threatened on every side by official persecution and popular fury, they had no opportunity for speculation on fundamentals--they pleaded merely to be allowed to live the life to which they were pledged. With the Eastern training, which most of them had had, so foreign to the ideals of Greek philosophy, and so tenacious of the idea of God, and with the person of Christ so near to them as to blind their eyes to the possibility of any other standard of truth than His words, they naturally afford us no material for the question under discussion.

Thus we must wait for the rise of Christian philosophy, and take as our ***terminus a quo*** the middle of the second century, when first there appears that literature which bears evidence to the conversion of philosophers to the Christian Church, and affords us examples of their attempts to present the new doctrines to the schools which they had abandoned.

Our *terminus ad quem* will be the Council of Nicea. The reason for this is in part the demands of time and space, and in part the fact that it will avoid needless and tedious repetition. The use of the theistic argument for some time after the Nicene period is fairly homogeneous, and presents no important new considerations. The apologetic work of the patristic writers was chiefly done in the ante-Nicene age; after that discussion turned more upon questions within the scope of the Christian Faith. The function of the age of the Councils was the formulation and definition of Christian dogma upon the admitted basis of the revelation of Jesus Christ.

This inquiry, therefore, will have to do with that interesting period when the doctrines of the Christian Church were finding their connection with and relation to the speculations of Greek philosophy, and when the Christian philosophers and apologists were determining the attitude which, for many centuries, revealed religion assumed toward the demonstrations of natural theology.

NOTES:
[1] *Philosophy and Theology*, p. 176.

CHAPTER II
GREEK AND ROMAN THEISTIC ARGUMENTS

The first question that confronts us as we enter upon the discussion is the preliminary inquiry: What had been done already in the way of theistic argument, and in what condition did the Christian Church find this argument when it first began to develop a system of apologetics? And from the conditions of ancient thought, or, at least, from what we know of it, this resolves itself into the question: How far had the Greek philosophers advanced by means of speculative thought toward a conscious theism, and by what means did the various individuals and schools among them seek to prove the existence of the Divine? The answer to this inquiry will involve a brief examination of the contributions of the pre-Socratic philosophers (especially Anaxagoras), Socrates, Plato, Aristotle, the Stoics, the Epicureans, Cicero, and the Hellenizing Jews of Alexandria.

The thought of Greece before the time of Socrates, from the very nature of its problem, and the material at its disposal, yields us but little that can, without doing violence to the facts, be construed as bearing on the theistic argument. The search of these early philosophers was, indeed, for an {Arche}, but their interest in the inquiry, as a perusal of the extant fragments of their writings will prove, was pre-eminently cosmological. They strove to discover the eternal ground of all things, but it was a principle to account for the phenomena of *physical* nature that they sought, and they had not attained to a realization of even a rude form of the theistic problem. All they sought for was a primary substance which should satisfy the needs of a rudimentary physical science, which would enable them to co-ordinate the scanty data which they had accumulated from their contact with the world in which they lived, and to whose secrets they seem at times, in spite of their limited knowledge, to have come very close. And even granting that the problem involved in their search for the {Arche} was at bottom identical with that of theism, they attempt to give no proof or argument for their conclusions with regard to it. They are as yet merely ***seers***, who report the vision that comes to them as they gaze upon the stress and strain and ever-changing spectacle of earth's phenomena. Even the teleology of Anaxagoras (often mentioned as the germ of the theistic argument) gives us nothing more than a poet's dream, expressed, as Diogenes Laertius informs us, in a "lofty and agreeable style."[2] "Nous," Anaxagoras tells us, "is infinite and self-ruled, and is mixed with nothing, but is alone, itself by itself.... It has all knowledge about everything, and the greatest strength; and Nous has power over all things, both greater and smaller, that have life. And Nous had power over the whole revolution, so that it began to revolve in the beginning.... And Nous set in order all things that were to be and that were, and all things that are not now, and that are, and this revolution in which now revolve the stars and the sun and the moon and the air and the aether that are separated off."[3] This, however, amounts to no argument, and it is extremely doubtful whether Anaxagoras ever meant anything more by his Nous than Empedocles did by his Love and Strife, of which it was the historical successor, and we may safely, I think, endorse the judgment of Aristotle when he says that "Anaxagoras, also, employs mind as a machine" (*i.e.*, as the Laurentian MS.

indicates, as a theatrical ***deus ex machina***) "for the production of the cosmos; and when he finds himself in a perplexity as to the cause of its being necessarily so, he then drags it in by force to his assistance; but, in the other instances, he assigns as a cause of the things that are being produced, everything else in preference to mind (Nous)."[4] This criticism will, I am confident, apply fully as well to any apparent theism in the other pre-Socratic writers,[5] so that we shall be justified in assigning to them as their part in the development of the theistic argument, the mere undefined feeling and growing conviction of a permanent behind the changing, a "one" behind the "many."

We find the natural deep and practical piety of Socrates reinforcing itself with a very full and complete statement of a teleological argument, based upon final cause, or adaptation of means to ends. It is in the ***Memorabilia***[6] that we get the clear statement of this, and, therefore, it is a Socratic teaching which can, fortunately, be definitely distinguished from the Platonic treatment of the subject. "But which," he asks, "seemed to you most worthy of admiration, Aristodemus--the artist who forms images void of motion and intelligence, or one who has the skill to produce animals that are endued not only with activity, but understanding?" Then as Aristodemus answers, "The latter," Socrates proceeds to a detailed description of the adaptations of the eye, ear, teeth, mouth and nose to their several uses, and concludes with the question: "And canst thou still doubt, Aristodemus, whether a disposition of parts like this should be a work of chance, or of wisdom and contrivance?" He also argues in like manner from the existence of intelligence in man, the soul, and the general adaptability of man's powers and conditions to the furthering of his life. This argument to design has appropriately been called "peculiarly the Socratic proof,"[7] and to his treatment of it, so in keeping with the practical, sturdy common-sense of the man, nothing essential or important, except in multiplication of applications and details, has been added since his time. In the opinion of the writer, however, Socrates, so far as one can judge from his recorded utterances, developed merely the form of the Argument to Design, but it cannot be positively asserted that he used it as a ***theistic*** argument. In the ***Memorabilia*** it is always "the gods" to which the argument leads, and the worship of them that he urges. He may have had a more theistic conception, but the context warrants no further meaning of {theos} than the generic one of an object of worship--in this case the national gods. In the *Apology* "{ho theos}" is used almost invariably of the local divinity of the oracle at Delphi, and of the "daemon" which, at the instigation of the Delphian divinity, as he was convinced, guided his actions. The present writer is strongly of the opinion that much violence has been done the words of Socrates by translators and interpreters, and that this fact will account for much of the alleged theistic teaching which is, without warrant, ascribed to the Athenian sage.

The contribution of Plato to the theistic argument was, characteristically, the form of the "Ontological proof" which has been called "Idealogical." This process is a very natural development for Plato's Dialectic.[8] Once divide the universe, as he did, into the two classes of permanent existence and transient phenomena, and identify the former with the ideas (which are nothing else than universals, each of which expresses the essence of many phenomena), and it is a very easy process to conceive of these ideas themselves being united in another more inclusive idea, and so, by a process of generalization, to reach at length the "Idea of Ideas"--the absolute Idea, in which lies the essence of all in the universe. Thus from any one fact of beauty, harmony, etc., the human mind may rise to the notion of a common quality in all objects of beauty, etc.: "from a single beautiful body to two, from two to all others; from beautiful bodies to beautiful sentiments, from beautiful sentiments to beautiful thoughts, until, from thought to thought, we arrive at the highest thought, which has no other object than the perfect, absolute, Divine Beauty."[9] The "ideas," too, and especially the "Good" or "absolute Idea," have in them a teleological element, "since the Idea not only states as what, but also for what a thing exists."[10] The absolute Idea is not only the first principle of the universe, but also its final purpose, and thus we have indicated in various places a teleological argument. Traces of other forms of the theistic argument have been detected in Plato's writings, but none of them are at all explicitly developed, and one cannot but feel that some writers on the subject have claimed altogether too much for Plato's theology.[11] The poetical and allegorical form into which he so constantly throws his discussion makes it extremely difficult to determine his exact position, especially on such a subject as his theology, in which he is constantly adapting his metaphysical doctrines to the prevailing polytheistic religious ideas; and at the same time this method of expression gives a good opportunity for the collection of isolated quotations which may support almost any theory.

The religious character of Plato's philosophy is, as Zeller says, to be found much more on the moral than on the scientific side, and hence he was content to leave the more exact formulation of such arguments as these to his successors. As to the results to which this method led him, the statement of Zeller, in view of the many conflicting opinions, seems satisfactory: "In everything that he states concerning the Divinity the leading point of view is the idea of the Good, the highest metaphysical and ethical perfection. As this highest Idea stands over all ideas as the cause of all being and knowing, so over all gods, alike hard to find and to describe, stands the one, eternal, invisible god, the Framer and Father of all things."[12] Of the personality of God Plato had no conception,[13] and it would be a very difficult undertaking to prove from his extant works that he was, in any real sense of the word, a theist.

Of the three divisions of the speculative sciences--physical, mathematical and theological--Aristotle makes the last the "most excellent,"[14] "for it is conversant about that one amongst entities which is more entitled to respect than the rest."[15] It is to the discussion of this subject in Book XI. that the greater part of the ***Metaphysics*** leads up. He has established in the previous portions of the work the two substances which he calls "natural or physical"--namely, matter and form--and now he proceeds to justify the hints he has given of a third substance which is "immovable."[16] It has been customary to divide this discussion of Aristotle into several formal theistic arguments,[17] but in the opinion of the writer the text of the ***Metaphysics*** does not lend itself readily to any such cut and dried arrangement of its argument. Aristotle does, indeed, to avoid the absurdity of an endless regress, argue from the {kinoumena} and the {kinounta} of the physical World to a {proton kinoun} which is a pure {energeia, akineton, aneu hyles}, and hence foreign to all the passivity and contingency of matter;[18] concludes from motion in the world that there must be a First Mover;[19] and asserts the actuality of the eternal as opposed to potentiality; but these arguments are so blended together, and take each one so much from the others, that I cannot be convinced that Aristotle had ever clearly differentiated them.

But it is clear enough that the crown of Aristotle's whole system is this "prime mover," "unmoved" and "apart from matter," and that this conception, up to which his thought leads from every side, as the necessary implication from the motion everywhere seen in the world, is his chief contribution to the argument for the existence of the Divine. Aristotle's chief interest lay in the cosmological problem, and his form of proof and the result which he reached by it were moulded by this fact. His argument did not lead him to a Creator of the world, for the universe, no less than the prime mover, was eternal, and the latter is nothing more than a principle of reason immanent in the world--pervading it, not distinguished from it--and the author of motion only in a passive way, after all, as a sort of magnetic object of desire.[20] In other places Aristotle makes passing references to different forms of the argument to prove the existence of the gods,[21] but it is evident that his own interest centered around this unmoved final cause, and it is in his proof of its existence from cosmological considerations that his significance for us lies.

In the post-Aristotelian schools we have an entire change of the point of view, and instead of a philosophy of nature, such as occupied the attention of the pre-Socratic thinkers, or a philosophy of mind, such as Socrates, Plato, and to a large extent, Aristotle attempted to construct, we find the interest of men in speculative questions centered in a philosophy of life, of morals. Corresponding to this change in the point of view, we may easily detect an alteration in the manner of dealing with the arguments for the existence of the gods.

There was, in the first place, an increased emphasis laid upon this line of thought, in common with religious subjects in general, and the reasons for the belief in the existence of the gods (for the Greek schools never transcended polytheism--when they speak of {theos} they mean simply the abstract divinity of the many separate divinities) seems, so far as we may judge from the comparatively scanty remains that have come down to us, to have been discussed at great length; critically and negatively by the Sceptics, positively and apparently with full conviction by the Stoics, and with a curious mixture of both of these attitudes by the Epicureans. These latter, if the reported doctrine of Epicurus himself be trustworthy, denied the popular gods, and, in order to insure freedom, rejected the Stoic doctrine of providence; but, on the other hand, asserted a belief in gods whose essential characteristics are immortality and perfect happiness (to insure which they must care nothing for the world or for men), and whose existence was held to be proven on the basis of the common consent of all men ("***Argumentum e Consensu Gentium***"). This argument is the result of a "natural idea" or "pre-notion," which Epicurus called {prolepsis};-

-"that is, an antecedent conception of the fact in the mind, without which nothing can be understood, inquired after, or discoursed on."[22]

The Stoics, on the other hand, with their strong conviction of providence working in the world, were rather inclined to deny the validity of this argument from common consent, and rested their belief in the gods, as Cicero makes his Stoic do in ***De Natura Deorum***,[23] on the evidence of design and purpose in the universe, but by this process succeeded only in proving to their own satisfaction that the world is divine--a fatalistic pantheism which roused the ire of the Epicurean and Sceptic alike, and which even Cicero seemed hardly to be able to accept.

From this necessarily brief review of the development of the argument for the existence of a Divinity in Greek and Roman thought, it will be seen that, at one time or another, in a more or less fully developed form, each one of the principal types of the theistic argument received the chief emphasis and had its method enunciated. The pre-Socratic natural philosophers, on the basis of the maxim as old as philosophy itself--{Adynaton ginesthai ti ek medenos prouparchontos}--pointed to an {Arche}--a real behind phenomena, a permanent behind the change--and thus pointed to the so-called Aetiological argument founded on the principle of causality. Socrates, with his pre-eminently practical disposition and ethical point of view, saw above all things intention in nature, and so from the consideration of this choice and adaptation of means to their end, and the resultant Final Cause he constructs a very complete Teleological argument for the existence of some intelligence behind the visible world. Plato's Ideas, as we have seen, determine the method by which he arrives at his abstract divinity, namely, by the "Idealogical" form of argument based upon a process of generalization. Aristotle, struck by the phenomena of motion in the universe, lays most stress on the course of reasoning which would lead back to the Prime Mover. The Epicureans, subordinating their theology to their ethical theory, and unwilling to allow their deity to interfere with the world or with men's affairs, developed and placed their dependence on the argument from common consent. The Stoics, laying great stress upon the order, proportion and harmony in the world, argued to mind as the reason for this condition of things. But none of these philosophers, in the opinion of the writer, attained to a conception of God which could in any real or accepted sense of the word be called theistic, or which would satisfy a mind accustomed to the idea of the Christian doctrine of God.

For the Greek writers never make any accurate distinction between {ho theos, hoi theoi, to theion} and {ta theia}. They never conceive of their {theos} as anything more than a rather larger and more majestic member of the innumerable family of the divinities of which the poets had sung--more spiritual only in so far as it was more vague and indefinite, a sort of mysterious, mythical being to which is sometimes attributed the same kind of personality possessed by the inferior gods, and sometimes regarded as simply the abstract divinity which characterized all of the gods. But that to which the arguments that we have been discussing generally lead is not even so near to the theistic conception as this modified polytheism, for they usually conduct us, as we have already indicated, to nothing more than a (sometimes) personified force of nature, principle of order, or abstract conception--not a God. Take away the inaccurate and misleading terms by which the original Greek is rendered in most of the English versions, in which the enthusiasm of the student of comparative religions has taken the place of the careful and accurate translator, and, aside from frequent apostrophes, such as are continually addressed by the poets to the many gods of the popular religion, the end of the arguments we have been considering will be found to be as depicted above. In a word: Greek philosophy, independent of Semitic influences, developed the *form* of the chief types of the theistic argument, but it failed utterly to deduce from them a theism, being throughout in its theology either polytheistic or pantheistic.

While considering this branch of our subject it would be impossible to ignore another school of thought, which, while neither Greek nor Roman in its nationality, yet derives so much of its philosophical stand-point from the former of these races as to be often classed under the same head. This is the school of Hellenizing Jews, in which there is built up on the foundation of the traditional faith of the Hebrew race, to the truth and authority of which they always held, a superstructure of philosophical speculation which follows closely the models afforded them by Greek thought. To effect a reconciliation between these two elements it was necessary for them to resort to the allegorical interpretation of the ancient inspired history of the race, and hence to the Oriental mind that wished to engage in speculative thought it was naturally Platonic and Pythagorean, rather than Aristotelian, methods that were most attractive.

The chief and probably the earliest developed example of this combination of

Oriental and Occidental thought is found in the writings of Philo Judaeus.[24] To him the powers of man seemed to be wholly unreliable and delusive, and only the special grace of God enables one to perceive any truth--"{Autos theos arche kai pege technon kai epistemon anomologetai}." To approach God one must flee from one's self--"{ei gar zeteis theon exelthousa apo sautes anazetei}." Neither reason nor any other function of the soul can conduct us to God, nor can we attain to a conception of Him as the supreme cause of all by regarding the manifold perfections and powers of nature, for such a process can give us only shadows. It is only by a "superior faculty" which is a grace of God that one can attain some idea of the divine, but even by this means we arrive at only negative knowledge--we can know only what God is not.[25] Yet in spite of all this Philo uses quite an elaborate teleological argument drawn from the order in the world.[26] This inconsistency, which, as Erdmann remarks,[27] may be explained by the fact that Philo makes God only the orderer of the world, and, furthermore, interposes an intermediate being, the famous Philonian Logos, we have thought it worth while to mention in this place, as it forms a connecting link between the Greek philosophers and the Alexandrian Fathers, and foreshadows, in some degree, the direction in which their thought was to be led.

NOTES:

[2] D. L., I, 16; II, 6.

[3] Ritter and Preller, 123. Translated by Burnet; **Early Greek Philosophy**, p. 283, 4.

[4] **Metaphysics**, I, 4.

[5] The "one god, the greatest among gods and men" of Xenophanes has led men to call him the first monotheist, but an examination of the fragments attributed to him will, I am sure, confirm the verdict of Burnet (**ut supra**, p. 123) that "what Xenophanes proclaimed as the 'greatest god' was nothing more nor less than what we call the material world."

[6] Xenophon: **Memorabilia**, I, 4.

[7] Cocker: ***Christianity and Greek Philosophy***, p. 491.

[8] "La dialectique et le systeme des idees conduisaient directement Platon a la demonstration de l'existence de Dieu; et son Dieu porte en quelque facon l'empreinte de cette origine, puisqu'il est a la fois l'unite absolue et l'intelligence parfaite." Jules Simon: ***Etudes sur la Theodicee de Platon et d'Aristote***, p. 29.

[9] ***Banquet***, Sec. 34.

[10] Erdmann: ***History of Philosophy***, Sec. 77, 4.

[11] E.g. Cocker: ***Christianity and Greek Philosophy***, pp. 377, ff.

[12] Zeller: ***Philosophie der Griechen***, II, i, s. 926.

[13] Plato "never raised the question of the personality of God." (Zeller; ***Greek Philosophy*** (briefer edition) Sec. 49.) "Sie" ("die Idee der Ideen") "ist natuerlich keine gottliche Persoenlichkeit." (Kahnis: ***Verhaeltniss der Alten Philosophie zum Christenthum***, p. 54.)

[14] ***Metaphysics***, V, 1.

[15] ***Ibid.***: x, 7.

[16] ***Metaphysics***, xi, 6.

[17] E.g., Schwegler: ***History of Philosophy***; Cocker; ***ut supra***, p. 412, ff.

[18] xi, 6.

[19] xi, 7.

[20] Jules Simon: ***Etudes sur la Theodicee de Platon et d'Aristote***, p. 88, ***et al.***; Davidson: ***Theism and Human Nature***, p. 45.

[21] Aristotle makes good use of the argument to design in a striking passage from a lost work quoted by Cicero in ***De Natura Deorum***, II, 37, and in ***Physica auscultatio***, II, 8, says: "The appearance of ends and means is

a proof of design."

[22] Cicero; ***De Natura Deorum***, I, 16, 17, and frequently. See also Seneca; ***Epist.***, cxvii, whose Syncretism allows him to borrow from Stoic and Epicurean alike. See also Zeller; ***Stoics, Epicureans and Sceptics***, p. 465.

[23] E.g., I, 36; II, 2, 5, ff.

[24] Vacherot: ***Histoire Critique de l'Ecole d'Alexandrie***, Vol. I, p. 142.

[25] ***Ibid.***: Vol. I, p. 143, 144.

[26] See e.g., the quotation in Stirling; ***Philosophy and Theology***, p. 173.

[27] ***History of Philosophy***, Vol. I, Sec. 114, 3.

CHAPTER III
THE PATRISTIC POINT OF VIEW

The philosophy of the Greeks during the first century of our era presents a great contrast to that of the age of Socrates, Plato and Aristotle. No longer do we find men engaged in the processes of positive, constructive thought, but we have presented to our view an age of retrospection, of literary criticism, and, to a great extent, of intellectual exhaustion. Men live amid the ruins of the systems constructed by their ancestors, and each one attempts to form for himself, out of the scattered fragments, a combination which may serve him as a sufficiently coherent rule of thought, and, especially, of life. Stoicism, Epicureanism, Scepticism, the "Orientalizing Hellenes," and the "Hellenizing Orientals," all by their restless, nervous, frequently erratic and aimless activity, bear witness to the fact that the mind of man has had revealed to it its own limitations, and is well on the way towards despair of ever arriving at truth. The Greek mind no longer exhibits that elasticity and spontaneity and enthusiasm in the search for truth, or that confidence in its results, which characterized the representatives of the best period of the thought of the race. The political fortunes of Greece do but typify the process which was going on in the Greek mind itself, and the period which we are considering is an age of intellectual as well as political decadence. This is manifested by the further fact that the thought of the age was largely turned backward and dwelt in the past. The day of original thought had passed by, and men were now content to deal with ideas at second hand--to be commentators rather than creators. This literary character which Greek philosophy now first began to exhibit was often seen and protested against. Thus Epictetus says: "If I study philosophy with a view only to its literature, I am not a philosopher, but a litterateur; the only difference is that I interpret Chrysippus instead of Homer."[28] But protest as they might, the inexorable signs of old age crept over the nation as irresistibly as they do over the individual, and, like the venerable man, preserved beyond his generation, Hellas lived largely in the memories of the past.

The influence of this condition of things is seen in the education of the times. The Greek world of this period, as we know it, was pre-eminently educated, but in a special, literary sense of the term. The foundation of their education was Grammar--the "Belles Lettres" of modern times. Sextus Empiricus says, "We are all given over to Grammar from childhood, and almost from our baby-clothes."[29] After Grammar came Rhetoric, "the study of literature by the study of literary expression and quasi-forensic argument,"[30] and Rhetoric was followed by Philosophy, which, however, like the other branches of study, so partook of the characteristics of the age that we find Marcus Aurelius congratulating himself in this manner: "I owe it to Rusticus that I found the idea of the need of moral reformation, and that I was not diverted to literary ambition, or to write treatises on philosophical subjects, or to make rhetorical exhortations."[31]

This saying of the imperial Stoic suggests another characteristic of the thought of the age--its ethical cast. From the time of Aristotle men had been content to have, to a large extent, the abstract problems of Ontology, Epistemology, and the others, and to lay emphasis on questions of life and manners. Stoicism, Epicureanism, Scepticism, and all the minor schools of the age, are pre-eminently ethical in their character. To be sure it was ethical theory rather than practice with which they were busied, but this fact makes the characteristic none the less important for the student of the history of philosophy.

This disorganized condition of thought which we have been attempting to depict has been well described by Dr. Stirling: "The fall of the old world, which was at once political, religious and philosophical, was characterized by a universal atomism. Politically, the individual, as an atom, found himself alone, without a country, hardly with a home. Religiously, the individual, as an atom, has lost his God; he looks up into an empty heaven; his heart is broken, and he is hopeless, helpless, hapless, in despair. Philosophically, all is contradiction; there is no longer any knowledge he can trust. What the world is he knows not at all. He knows not at all what he himself is. Of what he is here for, of what it is all about, he is in the profoundest doubt, despondency and darkness. Politically, religiously and philosophically thus empty and alone, it is only of himself that the individual can think; it is only for himself that the individual must care. There is not a single need left him now--he has not a single thought in his heart--but {eu prattein}, his own welfare."[32]

It was in the midst of this lump of Eclecticism, Syncretism and Scepticism that the leaven of Christianity was deposited, and the result of the fusion which took place after the first antagonism had passed away, makes this period a turning-point in the history of philosophy, and of the utmost importance as regards its effects on subsequent thought.

And of this antagonism and subsequent reconciliation, the early Christian Apologists were concrete examples. They had most of them, before they became Christians, been adherents of one or the other of the different philosophical sects, and several of them had tried all in turn.[33] They exemplified well the prevailing restless distrust of the results and methods of the older schools, but in Christianity--the belief in a Person, who was for them "the Way, the Truth and the Life"--they finally found the certainty for which they had so long sought in vain. The effect of this process, and of this result upon the attitude of the early Christian philosophers, could be none other than an increased distrust of the arguments for the existence of God, and an inclination to ignore them completely. These already suspected processes of reasoning by which the Greeks had been able to attain only to an abstract principle, or force, or mechanical cause, or arranger of the world, must be of very small importance to these men, upon whose sight had burst all at once, in the height of their despair, the vision of the Christian doctrine of God, certified to by one

The Basis of Early Christian Theism

whom they believed to be the veritable Son of God, "of one substance with the Father," and whose testimony to the truth of any fact brought a certainty which was infinitely superior to that which could be attained by any rational argument on other grounds. The transcendent authority of the teaching of Jesus Christ for these men, suddenly rescued by a belief in His claims from an absolute scepticism which was rapidly overflowing their minds, needs to be thoroughly appreciated before one can understand the position which they assumed, especially with reference to such a question as the one under discussion.

But though this basis of belief was sufficient for them, yet, as the primary mission of the Christian was to "go, disciple all nations," they were soon brought, in their endeavors to fulfil this command, into contact with those who not only denied the authority of their Teacher, but who were sceptical about the very fundamentals of religious belief. For the sake of these, then, and occasionally for the further confirmation of the faith of believers, and for purposes of illustration, the patristic writers return again to the discussion of those elements of belief for which they themselves felt no need, and hence we have in their works a rather frequent reference to the various forms of the theistic argument; but one which is evidently only incidental to their main course of thought, and which is brought in merely in accommodation to the needs of their readers. The ordinary arguments to prove the existence of God were not at all an essential, or even prominent, feature of early Christian Theology. And because of this secondary and incidental position of these arguments, they were never, as we shall see, given definite, conventional shape in the patristic use of them, nor were the various forms of the argument differentiated; but they were used in what we may call a mixed form, a combination of two or more different forms being put forth as one composite whole.

Besides these general influences which shaped the patristic treatment of the theistic arguments, we should notice certain fundamental and characteristic principles assumed by the Fathers, or by most of them, which have their bearing on our subject.

In the first place it is held by most of the early Christian authors, and explicitly stated by many of them, that the idea of the existence of God is innate in man as a "natural opinion." We have already noticed the doctrine of {prolepsis} advanced by Epicurus, and the somewhat similar position assumed by Philo, and we are not surprised to find that this idea took a strong hold on the devout minds of the early Christians. Thus St. Justin Martyr states that "the appellation 'God' is not a name, but ***an opinion*** ({prosagoreuma}) ***planted in the nature of man*** of a thing that can hardly be explained,"[34] and makes one of his discussions conclude that souls "can perceive ({noein}) that God exists."[35] St. Clement of Alexandria goes even further and affirms that "the Father, then, and Maker of all things is apprehended by all things, agreeably to all, ***by innate power and without teaching***."[36] Tertullian thinks that "the soul was before prophecy. From the beginning the knowledge of God is the dowry (***dos***) of the soul,"[37] and among the "things known even by nature" is "the knowledge of our God" which is "possessed by all,"[38] so that he could write a treatise, ***De Testimonio Animae***, and exclaim, "O noble testimony of the soul by nature Christian."[39] Origen speaks of "the uncorrupted idea of Him which is implanted in the human mind,"[40] and St. Cyprian makes this knowledge so plain that "this is the very height of sinfulness to refuse to acknowledge Him whom you cannot but know."[41] Arnobius, too, in a passage in which much allowance must be made for rhetorical fervor, exclaims, "Is there any human being who has not entered on the first day of his life with an idea of that Great Head? In whom has it not been implanted by nature, on whom has it not been impressed, aye, stamped almost in his mother's womb even, in whom is there not a native instinct, that He is King and Lord, the ruler of all things that be? In fine, if the dumb animals even could stammer forth their thoughts, if they were able to use our languages; nay, if trees, if the clods of the earth, if stones dominated by vital perceptions were able to produce vocal sounds, and to utter articulate speech, would they not in that case, with nature as their guide and teacher, in the faith of uncorrupted innocence, both feel that there is a God, and proclaim that He alone is Lord of all?"[42] Such language as this last example is, of course, the exclamation of the orator rather than the deliberate judgment of the philosopher, but taken in connection with the other passages cited it will indicate how strong a hold this conviction had on the Fathers, and will anticipate, to some extent, what we shall have to say later as to the use of the ***Argumentum e Consensu Gentium***.

In direct connection and sharp contrast with this opinion of the Fathers, there stands the seemingly contradictory statement, as frequently encountered in their writings, that the soul of itself cannot see God nor attain to true religion. In the very same sentence in which St. Justin Martyr asserts that souls "can perceive ({noein}) that God exists," he states that they do not see ({idein}) God,[43] and insists in more than one place that "neither by nature nor by human conception is it possible for men to know things so great and divine."[44] Frequently the patristic writers have occasion to emphasize the inability of man to attain by any of his natural powers to religious truth, and to point to the impotent longings and aspirations of Greek philosophy as an example of this. St. Clement of Alexandria, for example, asserts that "the chiefs of philosophy only guessed at" religious truth,[45] and lays down the general principle that "God, then, being not a subject for demonstration, cannot be the object of science."[46] Origen, too, states that "for ourselves, we maintain that human nature is in no way able to seek after God, or to attain a clear knowledge of Him without the help of Him whom it seeks."[47]

The inconsistency between these two fundamental positions of the Fathers, of which much is often made, is, I think, more apparent than real. For they make a clear distinction in their thought, though the mere language which they use is sometimes confusing, between knowledge of the existence of God--the undefined feeling or belief that there is a God--which is the "innate opinion," for which they give every man credit; and the knowledge of God, *i.e.*, of His attributes, etc., the subject-matter of dogmatic theology. The existence of the former of these, it is true, as of the latter, may be obscured and nearly obliterated by sin and the consequent disorganization; for in the teaching of the Fathers, as in that of their Master, it is the pure in heart that see God,[48] and it is only the man whose nature is kept in due balance by a life of moral rectitude--the "righteous man" of the Scriptures-- who can be expected to exhibit clearly this "natural opinion" or to attain to a full knowledge and appreciation of the Christian doctrine of God. At the very best, the knowledge of the Deity attained apart from revelation seemed to the Fathers to be, in comparison with their own certainty, miserably vague and conjectural, and they are constantly contrasting, in the most striking and graphic way, the contradictory and uncertain results to which the philosophers attained with the definiteness and consistency of the already well-defined doctrine of the Christian church. To them certainty in regard to knowledge of God can only come by means of the testimony of one who had seen and known,[49] and this testimony they are satisfied that they find in two places chiefly--first, in the testimony of the Prophets of the Old Testament, and, second, but in fact primarily, in the life and words of Jesus Christ, "the Word."

Of the antiquity and reliability of this first source--the Prophets--they were never tired of talking, and they were so confident of the necessity of resorting to it that they developed their famous theory of the indebtedness of Plato and Aristotle to those Hebrew seers for their theology. "From every point of view, therefore," concludes St. Justin Martyr, "it must be seen that in no other way than only from the prophets, who teach us by divine inspiration, is it at all possible to learn anything concerning God and the true religion."[50]

But the chief source from which the Fathers drew that certainty which they could not find in the demonstrations of philosophy was in the teaching of the Word, Jesus Christ. God, indeed, as we have seen, is not an object of science, "but the Son is wisdom and knowledge and truth, and all else that has affinity thereto. ***He is also susceptible of demonstration and of description.***"[51] It is in the incarnate Word of God that the patristic writers find expressed all that man is able to comprehend, and all that he needs to know in this present world, of the Divine Nature, and it is His words that confirm their confidence in that "innate opinion" of the existence of God, of the presence of which in every man they were so sure.

The subject of the "demonstration" of the existence of God is spoken of at some length in several places by St. Clement of Alexandria, and with his position most of the Fathers agree in the main. He regards the subject largely from an Aristotelian point of view. All knowledge is derived from Sensation and Understanding. "Intellectual apprehension is first in the order of nature; but in our case, and in relation to ourselves, Sensation is first, and of Sensation and Understanding the essence of knowledge is formed, and evidence is common to Understanding and Sensation."[52] But "should any one say that knowledge is founded on demonstration" (which "depends on primary and better known principles,"[53] being "discourse agreeable to reason, producing belief in points disputed, from points admitted"[54]) "***by a process of reasoning***, let him hear that first principles are incapable of demonstration, for they are neither by art" ({techne}), which is "practical solely, and not theoretical," "nor by sagacity" ({phronesis} = practical wisdom), which is "conversant about objects which are susceptible of change,"[55] but are "primary," "self-evident," and "indemonstrable."[56] Thus this "demonstration by a process of reasoning," apart from Sensation *and* Understanding, is only "to syllogize;" "for to draw the proper conclusion from the premises is merely to syllogize. But to have also each of the premises true is not merely to have syllogized, but also to have demonstrated," "so that if there is demonstration at all, there is an absolute necessity that there be something that is self-evident, which is called primary and indemonstrable."[57] On the basis of this theory of knowledge, it is evident that the usual arguments for the existence of God would have but little weight. For they either attempt to attain their end by formal thought alone, and thus result in mere "syllogizing;" or, starting from valid enough premises, they try to extend the conclusion beyond the limits imposed by the laws of "demonstration." For St. Clement, then, God is not "apprehended by the science of demonstration." If the Deity is to be known, there must be some place in which a union of the material and formal elements of "demonstration" of His existence is to be found. This he places in the life and teaching of Jesus Christ, who, as God incarnate, furnishes the "evidence" which "is common to Understanding and Sensation," and thus translates the "Infinite" and "Ineffable" into terms of the finite and comprehensible. In this paradox Christian theology has ever since been content to rest as one of the fundamental mysteries of the Faith.

But even with all the aids of revelation, the Fathers would not claim that man can advance to a full or adequate knowledge of God--we can simply know so much *about* God as is necessary for *practical* purposes--for ascertaining our proper end and duties. God is, from the very limitations of the human mind, "ineffable," "incomprehensible," "the unknown;"[58] and St. Clement of Alexandria expressly states even the best knowledge of God that man can by any means attain is only negative.[59]

These general positions, which in their broad lines are common to practically all of the Ante-Nicene Fathers, serve to confirm the historical interpretation of the place occupied by early Christian theistic thought, and will pave the way to an appreciation of their use of the arguments for the existence of God.

NOTES:

[28] ***Enchiridion***, 49.

[29] *Adversus Grammaticos*, I, 44.

[30] Hatch: *Hibbert Lectures*, 1888, Lect. II, where a full account is given of the education of the time, and what it signified.

[31] I, 7.

[32] *Philosophy and Theology*, p. 164.

[33] See e.g., St. Justin Martyr: *Dialogue with Trypho*, II.

[34] *Second Apology*, VI.

[35] *Dialogue with Trypho*, IV (end).

[36] *Stromata*, V, 14.

[37] *Against Marcion*, I, 10.

[38] *Resurrection of the Flesh*, III.

[39] *Apology*, XVII.

[40] *Against Celsus*, II, 40.

[41] *Treatise* VI, Sec. 9. See, also, Tertullian: *Apology*, XVII; "And this is the crowning guilt of men that they will not recognize One of whom they cannot possibly be ignorant."

[42] *Against the Heathen*, I. 33.

[43] *Dialogue with Trypho*, IV, "Even Homer distinguishes simple seeing ({idein}) from {noein}, which implies perception by the mind as consequent upon sight."

[44] *Hortatory Address to the Greeks*, V.

[45] *Exhortation to the Heathen*, XI.

[46] *Stromata*, IV, 25. In V, 12, he explains what he means by "demonstration": "Nor any more is He apprehended by the science of demonstra-

tion, for it depends on primary and better known principles. But there is nothing antecedent to the Unbegotten."

[47] ***Against Celsus***, VII, 20. See also VII, 44, and Clem. Alex.: ***Stromata***, II, ii, 4, and often.

[48] E.g., Theophilus (I, 1, 2) replies to the demand: "Show me thy God," by the counter-demand: "Show me ***yourself***, and I will show you my God."

[49] E.g., St. Justin: ***Hortatory Address***, V.

[50] ***Ibid.***, XXXVIII. See also V, VIII, and Athenagoras: ***Embassy***, VII; Clem. Alex.: ***Exhortation to Heathen***, VI, XI; ***Stromata***, I, 13; II, 2, 11; V, 14; Tertullian: ***Apology***, XVIII; Methodius: ***Miscellaneous Fragments***, 1.

[51] St. Clem. Alex.: ***Stromata***, IV, 25. For a few among many references, see: St. Irenaeus: ***Against Heresies***, V, i, 1; St. Clem. Alex.: ***Exhortation to Heathen***, XI; ***Instructor***, I, 12; ***Stromata***, I, 5, 19; II, 2; V, 1, 6, 11-13; VII, 1; VI, 5; Tertullian: ***Against Marcion***, V, 16; ***Against Praxeas***, XIV; Origen: ***De Principiis*** I, iii, 1; ***Against Celsus***, VII, 42, 44; Novatian: ***De Trinitate***, VIII; Arnobius: ***Against the Heathen***, I, 38.

[52] ***Stromata***, II, 4: "{ek de aistheseos kai tou nou he tes epistemes synistatai ousia koinon de nou te kai aistheseos to enarges}." The student of Kant's ***Kritik der Reinen Vernunft*** will find a number of familiar passages in St. Clement.

[53] ***Ibid.***, V, 12.

[54] ***Ibid.***, VIII, 3.

[55] ***Ibid.***, II, 4.

[56] ***Ibid.***, VIII, 3.

[57] ***Stromata***, VIII, 3.

[58] E.g., Theophilus: ***To Autolycus***, I, 3; St. Clem. Alex.: ***Stromata***, V, 12.

[59] ***Stromata***, V, 12: "If, then, abstracting all that belongs to bodies and things called incorporeal, we cast ourselves into the greatness of Christ, and then advance into immensity by holiness, we may reach somehow to the conception of the Almighty, ***knowing not what He is, but what He is not***."

CHAPTER IV
PATRISTIC USE OF THE THEISTIC ARGUMENTS

From this account of the general attitude of the ante-Nicene writers toward a possible knowledge of God, it will readily be anticipated that the forms of the theistic argument used by Plato and by Aristotle will find no place in their system. St. Clement of Alexandria, in a passage already referred to,[60] shows that any Ontological or Ideological argument can only lead us to an "Unknown," which may be "understood" and given meaning "by the Word alone that proceeds from Him;" and he and others of the early Christian writers seem to hint at that distinction between Epistemology and Ontology which has always been the chief enemy of any purely rational theistic argument. The Aetiological argument, too, is not explicitly stated by them; and, though Lactantius does, in opposing atheistic atomism, ask the question, "Whence are those minute seeds?" yet the casual character of the inquiry shows the small emphasis he placed on it, and the silence of the other writers, even when there was every opportunity for calling attention to such an argument, gives evidence to their estimate of its usefulness.

It is the more "practical" and "common-sense" forms of the theistic argument--the Cosmological, the Teleological, the argument from common consent, and mixtures of these types--that the early Christian writers use most frequently, and in this they do but conform to the general tendency of their age, as well as to the practical spirit of Christianity. As we have seen, the more artificial and abstract arguments of Plato and Aristotle did not take much hold upon others than their originators or formulators, and the distinct tendency of the theology of the later Greek and Latin schools of philosophy was toward the more concrete forms of the theistic argument. And this inclination would be emphasized in the early Christian writers, so far as they make use of the argument at all, by the eminently simple and common-sense attitude of Christianity toward all such problems, and also by the peculiar work which the primitive Church had to do in the conversion of the "common people," to whom an abstract argument would have been a waste of words.

But we should expect that to men, upon whom a close perusal and study of the Old Testament Scriptures had impressed the idea of God as the Creator, Law-Giver and Governor of the universe, the Cosmological argument would appeal strongly. Moreover, the strong Stoic influence which is seen in their works, particularly in their treatment of questions of morals, and in their ethical terminology, would naturally, one would think, pre-dispose them to regard with favor this argument, so in vogue among the philosophers of the Porch. It is, therefore, all the more remarkable that, among the important works of the Ante-Nicene Fathers, not more than a dozen instances, at most, of this argument can be found; and of these more than half are merely passing references to the patent fact of order in the world. Thus Tertullian asserts (quite incidentally, in the course of an argument on an ethical question), that "Nature herself is the teacher" of the fact "that God is the Maker of the universe,"[61] but even here it is doubtful whether he means to appeal to order or design in the world. In another place he makes the mere statement that the fact of God's existence is tested by His works; His character by the beneficence of them;[62] in another that the "Creator ought to be known even by nature;"[63] and in still another that nature teaches all men the existence and character of God.[64] Origen in a passage sometimes quoted, appeals to the order and harmony of the world,[65] but it is to prove the unity of God rather than His existence. Perhaps the best and most elaborate example of the use of the Cosmological argument by the Ante-Nicene authors, is that made of it by "Athenagoras the Athenian; Philosopher and Christian," as he styled himself.[66] He is concerned with making a distinction between God and matter, in opposition to the popular idolatry, and declares that Christians see the "Framer" behind the orderly world--whose relation one to the other he likens to that between the artist and the materials of his art. "But as clay cannot become vessels of itself without art, so neither did matter, which is capable of taking all forms, receive apart from God the Framer, distinction and shape and order."

And these few incidental and scattered instances represent practically the explicit use of the Cosmological argument in the writings with which we are occupied. When we consider how constantly they must have met with the statements of it which are prevalent in the writings of the Stoics, by whom they were, we know, profoundly influenced in both the form and the terminology of their thought, we must surely consider this omission a significant fact, for which it is worth while trying to account.

Nor does the "Socratic proof," the argument to design, meet with any more cordial reception at the hands of early Christian writers. Although the cases in which it is used are generally more explicit and fully developed, yet the appeals to design in nature are fewer even than those to order. The earliest, and one of the best examples of the use of this argument is that made by Theophilus, Bishop of Antioch, in his work addressed to the idolater Autolycus.[67] He seeks to prove that the invisible God is perceived through His works. As the soul is unseen, yet perceived through the motion of the body; as the pilot is inferred from the motion of the ship; as the king, though not present in person, is believed to exist from his "laws, ordinances and authorities;" so the unseen God is "beheld and perceived through his providence and works." "Consider, O man, His works," he exclaims; and proceeds to enumerate the evidences of design in the universe--"the timely rotation of the seasons," "the regular march of the stars," the various beauty of seeds and plants and fruits, and many others. It is a passage of considerable beauty, and evidences no mean rhetorical skill.

It is in this same connection--in the refutation of idolatry--that St. Clement of Alexandria uses this argument, contrasting the living organism of man with the heathen idols.[68] "None of these (artists) ever made a breathing image, or out of earth moulded soft flesh. Who liquefied the marrow? or who solidified the bones? who stretched the nerves? who distended the veins? who poured the blood into them? or who spread the skin? who ever could have made eyes capable of seeing? who breathed spirit into the lifeless form? who bestowed righteousness? who promised immortality? The Maker of the universe alone; the great Artist and Father has formed us, such a living image as man is. But your Olympian Jove, the image of an image, greatly out of harmony with truth, is the senseless work of Attic hands." This, it will be readily seen, is more an attempt to show the insufficiency of idolatry to account for man's nature, than a deliberate attempt at theistic proof.

The other examples of the use of this form of the argument for the existence of God are found in Lactantius, "the Christian Cicero." In speaking of Socrates he introduces[69] with approval an epitome of the Athenian sage's argument, which we have already considered,[70] and, in combatting the atomistic theory of the origin of the world, he asserts[71] that neither atoms nor the "Nature" of Lucretius can account for the adaptations in the actual world; and the phenomena of mind, especially, proclaim an intelligent Providence. His treatise "On the Workmanship of God, or the Formation of Man," is almost entirely an argument to design from the phenomena of man's physical and mental nature. From the standpoint of the physiology and psychology of his time, he discusses in detail the function and working of the different parts of man's nature, and from the adaptation of means to ends, of organs to their functions, which, even with the scanty data of the science of that day, is a striking consideration, he concludes that man's being can only be accounted for on the supposition of an Arranger or Planner, whose purposes are carried out in exercise of the various functions.

The argument *e Consensu Gentium* has often been accredited with being peculiarly the patristic argument for the existence of God,[72] and for this conclusion the use of it in Epicurean theology, and the doctrine of the natural, innate idea of God already considered, would fully prepare us; but the fact is that, apart from frequent passing references to the "natural opinion" mentioned in the preceding chapter, the instances in which the argument is explicitly made use of are not much more numerous than in the case of the other forms. They constantly appeal to the common consent, but it is generally against polytheism, as indicating a consciousness of *the unity* of God. St. Justin Martyr, in the passage to which we have already alluded, asserts[73] this common consent, but only as preparatory to the certainty which he finds in revelation. St. Clement of Alexandria, after asserting that "the Father and Maker of all things is apprehended by all things, agreeably to all, by innate power, and without teaching," goes on to confirm his statement in this manner:[74] "But no race anywhere, of tillers of the soil, or nomads, and not even of dwellers in cities, can live without being imbued with the faith of a superior being. Wherefore, every eastern nation, and every nation touching the western shore; or the north, and each one toward the south--all have one and the same preconception respecting Him, who hath appointed government; since the most universal of His operations equally pervade all." It is with the principles and end of this argument in view that Tertullian appeals[75] to the witness of the soul, "not as when fashioned in schools, trained in libraries, fed in Attic academies and porticoes," but "rude, uncultured and untaught, such as they have thee who have thee only; that very thing of the road, the street, the workshop wholly;" and from his examination of this ordinary soul he concludes that "the knowledge of our God is possessed by all."[76] Minucius Felix appeals to this same common instinct and exclaims:[77] "What! is it not true that I have in this matter the consent of all men?" and Origen, in his reply to the attack of Celsus, points to "the ineradicable idea of Him."[78] Novatian asserts[79] that "the whole mind of man is conscious" of Him, "even if does not express itself," and Lactantius thinks that for Cicero "it was no difficult task, indeed, to refute the falsehoods of a few men who entertained perverse sentiments by the testimony of communities and tribes, who on this one point had no disagreement."[80]

Besides these instances in which the different types of the theistic argument are used in an undeveloped, but yet in a pure form, there are several places where a mixed form appears, the different conventional processes being used in combination without being clearly differentiated. Thus the argument from common consent and the argument based on order or design are used in conjunction, the necessity of the universal knowledge of God's existence being seen from the witness to Him found in nature.[81] So, too, the arguments from order and from design in nature are often used in conjunction, and in many passages it is difficult to decide to which one of these two the author intends to appeal primarily.[82] These undifferentiated or mixed arguments are quite frequently to be seen in the patristic writings, and serve to illustrate the eclectic character of their thoughts, often presenting in one passage the forms of the theistic arguments peculiar to two opposed schools in Greek philosophy; and they also indicate how incidentally and naively the Fathers used such weapons, not taking the trouble to differentiate one form from the other, though they could not have been ignorant of such distinctions.

The first thing that strikes one's attention in this examination of the use of the theistic argument in the early Christian writers is, as has been indicated, the paucity of examples. When we consider the emphasis laid upon this subject in the contemporaneous philosophical schools; the constant appeal to one form or another of the argument by Stoic and Epicurean alike; the various combinations and adaptations made by Eclectics and Syncretists; the use of such material in the exercises of the rhetorical instruction then so prominent in education; it would seem that a weapon so ready to their hand must have been seized upon by the Fathers, and made full use of for the advancement of the cause in which they were enlisted. And this silence on their part cannot be due to ignorance of what had been written on the subject, or of what was going on in the world about them. The patristic writings show the keenest interest in, and fullest knowledge of what men were thinking about in the outside world as well as within the Church. Many of the Fathers, as we have had occasion to notice, had been trained in the philosophical schools,[83] and show themselves fully conversant not only with such subjects, but with poetry and general literature as well.[84] In the course of their education, as well as in their reading, they must have become fully acquainted with all the forms of the theistic argument. And this knowledge they had every opportunity to use. Many of their works that have come down to us are either apologies or else answers to critics of Christianity, who attacked its doctrines from the stand-point of either polytheism or atheism. In maintaining the Christian doctrine of God against these opponents, the theistic argument would seem to be a most natural weapon for one who was confident of its validity. But the fact is, that in most of these apologies no such reasoning is employed, and even when it is to be found in their pages, is only incidental and by way of illustration, to explain the rational character of the Christian doctrine of God by a sort of ***argumentum ad hominem***.

One reason for this neglect of the theistic argument may be readily found in the subject-matter of the treatises themselves. Almost exclusively with the earlier Fathers, as we have seen, and very largely with their successors, the emphasis was laid on life, rather than on thought, and the appeal was to authority rather than to reason. Men were asked to judge of Christianity by its fruits, and to receive the faith which it professed, not because of its rational demonstration, but because of the authority of Him who promulgated it. The persons to whom the arguments were addressed, too, explain much of the silence of the Fathers. To the Jew or religious

Gentile it would be superfluous to address elaborate arguments to prove the existence of God, and it was to these classes that many of the works under discussion were addressed. To them the argument, such as we frequently find, from the Old Testament types and prophecies, or from the superior beauty and morality of the Christian doctrine and life, taking for granted the existence of God, was what the case required. And when, as is very frequently the case, they address the popular idolaters, it is a negative argument to show the unworthiness of idol-worship, and the superiority of their own doctrine, of which they naturally make use, and not a theistic argument which would have no significance to those who were already "too religious."

Many of the apologies of the early Church were called forth by the attacks which were made on the Christians by the adherents of the popular religions. The charges usually brought against them were those of atheism, because of their rejection of the gods of Greece and Rome; of immorality, because of the secrecy and mystery of their meetings, and cannibalism, because of their doctrine of the partaking of the Body and Blood of Christ in the Eucharist. In refuting these charges, especially the first, no place was afforded for the use of a theistic argument, but they naturally exhibit their belief in God as superior to that of their accusers, and appeal to their lives as justifying their belief.

But aside from these cases in which the theistic argument would have been superfluous, there are many places in which it is conspicuous for its absence. That they had other arguments besides those from scripture and authority, and that they believed in using them when necessary, we have, as we have seen, many proofs in their writings. Their position is well indicated by Lactantius, who blamed St. Cyprian for using a Scripture argument to an unbeliever,[85] and we shall be obliged to look deeper than mere ignorance or lack of occasion to account for the paucity of cases in which they use the argument for the existence of God.

The fact is that the history of Greek thought had shown conclusively the absolute futility of any efforts to arrive at a certain proof of the existence of God by purely rational methods. The attempts of each school to attain such certainty were repudiated by their successors, and even by their contemporaries; and the later trials--which the religious instincts and aspirations of men would not permit them to forego, even when they were sceptical of obtaining any valid and positive results--frequently became, instead of a sincere seeking after God, mere practice in the art of Rhetoric. And not only was it true that no one of the forms of the theistic argument brought conviction to any other mind than that of the man who regarded it with the partial enthusiasm of an originator or formulator, but even such an one was led to only the most vague and indefinite results. We have already seen how even the best theology of the Greeks led to nothing but a sort of organized or unified polytheism. A vague, fanciful first cause of physical phenomena, a general idea, abstracted out of all content, so as to leave no meaning for the human mind--whatever the imagination might make of it--a mechanical, magnetic force, to which all motion might conveniently be referred; a deified principle of order--and these held in conjunction with the popular polytheism, and impregnated with the national pantheistic conceptions--was all that Greek philosophy could offer to the higher religious aspirations of the educated man. The opinion of the Greek mind itself as to the character of the knowledge of God, to which the thought of their race had led them at the beginning of the Christian era was fitly expressed by those Athenians, who erected near the Areopagus the "altar on which was written, 'To the Unknown God.'"[86] The opinion (for in most cases it did not amount to a conviction) that there was an Unknown (or even, as many thought, an Unknowable) Divinity of some sort, which might account for the phenomena of the world, and which might be the truth behind the vagaries of the anthropomorphic polytheism, was as far as Greek thought had led men at the period with which we have to do. Their {theos} was really nothing more than Mr. Herbert Spencer's "Unknowable,"--a mysterious "force," to which everything was referred which could not be accounted for on the basis of scientific principles.

Now if this was the case with the adherents of the heathen philosophical schools, how must the realization of the poverty of this result, and the distrust of the means which led to it, have been emphasized by the conversion of individuals from them to Christianity. It is a graphic picture which some of the Fathers paint for us of their eager search, in the different schools in turn, for some religious truth which would bring with it conviction; of their disappointment and consequent despair and scepticism, and then of the satisfaction which they had found for their aspirations in the teaching of Jesus Christ, who, they were convinced, was the very Word of God. Viewed merely from the historical point of view, this process is full of interest as illustrating that which was going on in many minds that stopped at the sceptical stage, and, for one reason or another, never found refuge in the Christian Church. But for those who did take this step, their former distrust of the theistic argument, as a basis for religious conviction, must have been greatly emphasized. The contrast between their former scepticism as to man's ability to attain to any knowledge of things beyond the phenomenal world, and their present faith and conviction which their belief in the Person of Christ gave them, must have made the part of any such means of arriving at truth as the already discredited theistic argument most insignificant. They, themselves, had no need for it. All it had been able to do for them, as for those to whom they wrote, was to raise an aspiration which "would not down"--to bring them to the hypothesis (substituted for polytheism, now outgrown) of an "Unknown God," and they felt that their message to their contemporaries was, like that of St. Paul to the Athenians on Areopagus: "Whom, therefore, ye ignorantly worship, Him declare I unto you."

It is with this attitude in mind, I am convinced, that we must interpret the doctrine, so often enunciated by the early Christian writers, but especially by St. Justin Martyr and St. Clement of Alexandria, of the "partial," "fragmentary" character of the theological truth arrived at by Greek philosophy. They have sometimes been charged with inconsistency in thus characterizing the work of men from whom they borrowed so much, but they seem, in fact, to have been remarkably appreciative of their old masters when we consider the position in which they stood. In fact, they seem to grant to Greek philosophy all that its adherents would claim for it, namely, that, by means of the arguments adduced by its different schools, the Greeks had attained to the opinion that there was something behind the phenomena of nature, but this might as well be a transcendent force or a pantheistic world-soul as an immanent God. With the Apostle on Mars' Hill they would say that the best theology of the Greeks simply put them in a position "that they should seek the Lord, if haply they might feel after Him and find Him."

And each of the Greek schools, they would say, by resting their case on some one of the various arguments, and emphasizing some one of the attributes of the Deity at the expense of the others, had attained only a partial and inadequate view, though true so far as it went. "Since, therefore," says St. Clement of Alexandria,[87] "truth is one (for falsehood has ten thousand by-paths); just as the Bacchantes tore asunder the limbs of Pentheus, so the sects both of barbarian and Hellenic philosophy have done with truth, and each vaunts as the whole truth the portion which has fallen to its lot. But all, in my opinion, are illuminated by the dawn of Light." These men were deeply appreciative of the work of Greek philosophy so far as it went--even assigning to it a place analogous to the Hebrew Scriptures[88]--but they always attribute to it a distinctly propaedeutic office, and are careful to emphasize its failure to lead to any firm and positive conviction of the existence of God. That this was the position of the early Christian philosophers might be shown by many passages, but we will content ourselves with one example from the pages of St. Clement of Alexandria, who assigned to Greek philosophy a higher place than any of the patristic writers--so much so that his orthodoxy has frequently been questioned because of it. He is fond of designating the knowledge of God to which the Greeks had attained by the term "{periphrasis}." Thus he concludes[89] an argument from common consent, already quoted, in these words: "Much more did the philosophers among the Greeks, devoted to investigation, starting from the Barbarian philosophy, attribute providence to the 'invisible, and sole and most powerful, and most skilful and supreme cause of all things, most beautiful;'--not knowing the influences from these truths, unless instructed by us, and not even how God is to be known naturally, but only, as we have already often said, by a true periphrasis." "The men of highest repute among the Greeks knew God, not by positive knowledge, but by indirect expression ({periphrasis})."[90] The indefinite and merely "probable" character of the results which the Fathers think were reached by the theistic argument in Greek thought explains to us the few examples of these proofs which we find in their writings, and the certainty which they thought they had found, and their consequent attitude toward all arguments of this nature, which we have tried to depict, is the key to the explanation of a new phase in the history of thought which was to last for several centuries.

In our examination of these examples of the theistic argument in the Fathers, it cannot escape our notice that they occur much more frequently, and in more developed and conventional form in the West than in the East--under the influence of Rome than under that of Alexandria and the Orient. The reason for this is not far to seek, and is one that throws light also on the motive with which the patristic writers made use of these arguments.

In Alexandria and the East there was no incentive for the Christians to try to prove the existence of God, for the philosophy of that portion of the world was essentially religious in its character, and based its speculation on the existence of God as a fundamental postulate of revelation and of reason as well. In the combination of Judaism and Hellenic philosophy made by the "Hellenizing Jews" and by the "Judaizing Hellenes," the existence of God was admitted quite as freely, and maintained quite as zealously, as by the Christians themselves, and even the incipient Neo-Platonists made no quarrel with them on this ground. So we find that the reference in the Alexandrian and other Eastern Fathers are mainly of the character of examples and illustrations as to principles that are well understood and admitted, and are employed chiefly for the purpose of refuting idolatry by a distinction between God and matter, or of proving the unity of God in opposition to the still latent polytheism.

Under the influence of Rome, however, other tendencies came in to give a rather different significance to the theistic argument. For Rome had become the chief center of the later schools of Greek philosophy, and under the shadow of the seven hills rather than in the Athenian groves and porticoes were found the disciples of Pyrrho, of Zeno and of Epicurus. Thus, very naturally, wherever Roman civilization was dominant the teacher of Christian doctrine was obliged to present his subject with reference to the forces already at work in the minds of those whom he addressed. In accordance with this, we find, first, a ***negative*** influence in the hostile attitude assumed by the Sceptics and members of other schools who tended toward their position, toward any religious knowledge. That this influence is not an imaginary one may be seen especially in the instance already quoted from Lactantius, whose use of the theistic argument is called forth by the cavils of Sceptics and atheistic atomists.

But there was also a ***positive*** influence at work to facilitate the use of the theistic argument by the Western Fathers in the prevalence at Rome of Stoic and Epicurean doctrine. From the former of these schools would result a familiarity, and, in many cases, an agreement with the forms of the argument drawn from order and design; from the latter, for the demonstration from common consent. Both of these influences, no doubt, had some influence on the shape in which Tertullian of Carthage, Minucius Felix, Novatian and Lactantius presented their doctrine, and, together with the more material and less religious character of the West, accounts in large degree for the comparative frequency of their appeal to the theistic argument.

But when we consider the frequency with which we meet with the theistic argument, and with reference to its use in other writers, in the pages of Cicero, for example, these scanty instances afforded us by the writings of the ante-Nicene Fathers, whose works occupy, say, 4,500 large, closely-printed pages in the translation, and who were, let us remember, dealing exclusively with religious thought, indicate plainly a fundamental change in position, the influence of which was operative for centuries in this department of thought, and which, even to-day, governs the attitude of the greater part of the Western world. The absolute failure of the Greeks to arrive at any certainty of God's existence by demonstration, the introduction of the Christian doctrine of God, before which the deductions of Greek philosophy seem empty and unsatisfactory, even to many who cannot accept that doctrine as truth, and the substitution of faith in a Person for purely rational proof, render it impossible, so long as that faith continues, that any one should think it worth while to devote more than a passing notice to any such argument, unless for the purposes of an ***argumentum ad hominem***. And so it is not until faith begins to grow cold and men become mere speculators and debaters about religion, rather than believers in Christ, that the revival of these arguments under the title of "proofs" is possible. Even the famous Ontological Argument of St. Anselm was, I am convinced, no serious attempt to formulate an ***a priori*** proof of the existence of God, but was addressed to a particular case[91]--the "fool" who "said in his heart, 'There is no God,'" and who ***also*** maintained that God was "that than which no greater can be thought."

From this survey it will be seen that, in the view of the Ante-Nicene Christian authors, the theistic argument was valuable merely as a propaedeutic to Christianity, but was superfluous for the believer in Jesus Christ; the use of it cannot, as it had not in Greek thought, bring proof, but only probability; even this uncertain result is only vague and fragmentary in character, and was never unified and made significant by the Greeks; its office in Christian evidences was merely of an ***ad hominem*** sort, and this only in its simpler and more practical forms, in which the senses as well as reason had their testimony to bear; and, lastly, the argument was used much more frequently by the Western than by the Alexandrian and other Eastern Fathers.

NOTES:

[60] *Stromata*, V, 12.

[61] *De Spectaculis*, II.

[62] *Against Marcion*, I, 17.

[63] *Ibid.*, V, 16. This is to justify his doctrine of the punishment of the heathen.

[64] *Scapula*, II.

[65] *Against Celsus*, I, 23.

[66] *Plea for the Christians*, XV, XVI.

[67] I, 5 and 6.

[68] *Exhortation to the Heathen*, X.

[69] *Divine Institutes*, III, 20.

[70] Chap. II.

[71] *Treatise on the Anger of God*, X.

[72] E.g., Stirling: *Philosophy and Theology*, p. 179.

[73] *Trypho*, III, IV.

[74] *Stromata*, V, 14.

[75] *The Soul's Testimony*, I.

[76] *Of the Resurrection of the Flesh*, III.

[77] ***Octavius***, XVIII.

[78] ***Against Celsus***, II, 40.

[79] ***De Trinitate***, VIII.

[80] ***Divine Institutes***, I, 2.

[81] E.g., Irenaeus: ***Against Heresy***, II, 9, 1; Tertullian: ***Against Marcion***, I, 10; Origen: ***De Principiis***, I, 3, 1; Tertullian: ***Apology***, XVII; Lactantius: ***Divine Institutes***, I, 2.

[82] E.g., Minucius Felix: ***Octavius***, XVII, XVIII; Novatian: ***De Trinitate*** VIII; Dionysius the Great: ***Fragments***, II, 1.

[83] E.g., "Justin, in Philosopher's garb, preached the word of God." Eusebius, IV, 11.

[84] The mere list of Greek authors ***quoted*** by St. Clement of Alexandria occupies over fourteen quarto pages in Fabricius' ***Bibliotheka Graeca***.

[85] ***Divine Institutes***, V. 4.

[86] ***Acts***, XVII, 23.

[87] ***Stromata***, I, 13.

[88] E.g., ***Stromata***, VI, 5: "The one and only God was known by the Greeks in a Gentile way, by the Jews Judaically, and in a new and spiritual way by us." In I, 5, he says: "For this (philosophy) was a schoolmaster to bring "the Hellenic mind," as the law the Hebrews, to Christ."

[89] ***Stromata***, V, 14.

[90] ***Ibid.***, VI, 5. See also, e.g., I, 19; V, 13.

[91] See Stirling: ***Philosophy and Theology***, p. 35.

CHAPTER V
ECLECTIC THEISM

The early Christian writers, so far as they assumed any philosophical position, were invariably Eclectics. In this, as we have seen, they were the true children of their age, whose most striking characteristic was that it had deserted the older systems, while attempting to preserve out of their ruins the particular truth for which each of the schools had contended. But with the Christian philosophers it was not merely the negative influence of scepticism which drove them to Eclecticism. Their conviction of a sure knowledge of things divine--the final question for all philosophy--exerted a positive influence as well, which led them to formulate more or less explicitly a view of the function of philosophy as an organon of the truth, not merely with reference to the past history of Greek thought, as their contemporaries outside of the Christian Church were accustomed to do, but with a view to all possible speculation on the Deity. For this deposit of revealed truth, to which they gave assent as the most certain of all knowledge, they regarded as the ***whole*** truth, of which the various speculations of philosophy on the existence and attributes of God, were but "portions" and "fragments"--true and trustworthy so far as they went, and from their own particular standpoint, but, nevertheless, essentially and necessarily partial, and hence productive, not of certainty, but of mere opinion.

And this estimate of the function of philosophy with respect to theological truth, which the Fathers worked out on the basis of the concrete example of the course of Greek thought, though with a view to a much wider application, has its justification in the very nature and conditions of thought itself. For philosophy is essentially a ***process***--its very life depends on its being in motion, in process of change and development. Each system is evolved out of its predecessors, and contains within itself the germs of its successors--it is the link which connects the past with the future. It expresses the "common-sense," the unconscious convictions and instinctive tendencies of the time, and the man who first gives voice to this unspoken message is the philosopher. He utters the truth which the times demand--that which satisfies the conditions. Thus with Professor Erdmann[92] the patristic writers would say that each statement of philosophical truth is "the final truth only for that time." It is the phase or aspect or particular statement of the truth which the times demand, which the situation calls forth, and which appeals most strongly to the minds that make up part of that situation. Changed conditions demand a different statement of the truth to satisfy them, and furnish the data upon which such a statement is based. Philosophy, like science, "does not really accumulate, but is entirely transformed by each fresh hypothesis. It is only the data that accumulate; and when we say that a new hypothesis is 'truer' than that which preceded it, we mean merely that it enables us to co-ordinate a larger number of these data."[93] And this transformation takes place, in reality, not only by addition, but by subtraction of data. For it is a phenomenon common to the thought of all ages, that each school not only calls attention to new data, ignored by its predecessor, but also shuts its eyes to more or less of the valid data set forth by the earlier system. In no period of the history of thought were men more commonly led into abstractions by being dazzled by the brilliancy and novelty of the latest idea than in the pioneer age represented by Greek philosophy, when men had not yet attained to a clear perspective, and the foot-hills often hid the lofty mountain peak.

It is this trait, so evident in the naive thought of the Greeks, that makes it possible for the early Christian thinkers to take the attitude, at once appreciative and critical with regard to the Hellenic theology. They borrowed much, not only from the form, but also from the results of the speculations of the philosophers, but always with a deep sense of the limitations which the conditions imposed upon them. Socrates, Plato, Aristotle and the rest had spoken the truth, but each only from one point of view, and on the basis of only one method of approach. The conclusions of each were the result of a process of more or less complete abstraction, and in abstractions the Fathers, true to the genius of Christian thought, could never rest content, but could only accord to them the appreciation which belongs to a temporary and preliminary stage in the search for the final unity.

To this partial, temporary, "relatively final," and constantly changing content, the revealed doctrine of God, manifested in due relations, unity and completeness by the Incarnate Word, stands with the Fathers as the principle to the particular rule or application--as the whole to the part. As the revelation of God it came to them, not as the result of man's investigation and speculation, colored by every change of time, place and environment, a mere momentary phase of a process; but as eternal verity, viewed, so far as man's powers would allow, in its entirety and unity. Dorner expresses their position well when he says that in Christianity "as the organism of the truth, the elements of truth, elsewhere here and there to be met with in a scattered form or a disfigured guise, come together in unity--a unity which, as it personally appeared in the God-Man, so in the course of history ever more and more rises upon the consciousness of mankind." The Fathers think that in the Christian doctrine of God they find all the true elements contributed by previous thought, and besides these an infinite depth of truth unthought of by the Greeks, all unified and harmonized in a way that makes it a sharp contrast to the fragmentary and abstract character of the Hellenic theology. Christian doctrine represents to them the stable, absolute truth, so far as it was revealed by the Incarnate Word, the eternal verities in their completeness and unity, so far as man is able to comprehend them. Philosophy represents the phase or aspect of the truth which the conditions of thought at the time demands and emphasizes, which will co-ordinate the data at present in the foreground of consciousness. Thus they conceive of the facts of Christian Theology as the goal towards which philosophy is (often unconsciously) striving, but at which it can never arrive without the "leap of faith." Once this leap is taken, however, these theological verities become the major factors in the data to be co-ordinated, and philosophy and theology come into that union and harmony which, in the eyes of the Christian philosophers, is their normal relation.

This Eclectic attitude of the Fathers, and their deprecation of any abstraction or partial statement usurping the place of the truth, explains to some extent their treatment of the theistic argument.

In the first place it led them to distrust and reject any argument for the existence of God which proceeded on the basis of reason alone, apart from any content furnished by sensibility. While the Fathers do not make any explicit and scientific distinction between Epistemology and Ontology, such as has in modern times been the bane of any attempted natural theology, yet they seem to have made a pretty constant *practical* separation between the two. St. Clement of Alexandria, as we have seen, holds that by a method of abstraction of specific characteristics we can arrive only at an "Unknown," to which meaning can be given only by combining with this rational process some content furnished directly by the senses or, indirectly, by testimony, and he further states that God is not a subject for demonstration--*i.e.*, the science that depends on primary and better known principles--for "first principles are incapable of demonstration."[94] This position seems to be tacitly assumed by the patristic writers throughout, and even where they speak of Plato with gratitude and admiration they never seem to be at all inclined to make any use of his "Ideological" argument or anything related thereto. They seem to take a common-sense stand for the testimony of the whole man, as well as for the whole truth, and to instinctively distrust any rational concept in the formation of which sensuous content had been ignored.

The Eclectic character of the patristic thought is seen also in the frequency with which they use the different forms of the theistic argument in conjunction, or present it in mixed forms. The Greek philosophers, as we have seen, each selected some one of the forms of the argument, and by means of it, attempted to establish the sort of an {Arche}, to which such a course of reasoning would lead, ignoring, or attacking the forms in use by their rival school. Thus early, however, as in modern times, Christian theology, in contrast with the attempts of rational theology, began to emphasize the interdependence of these different forms of the theistic argument, and the cumulative character of their evidence. Each one of itself could bring no conviction, nor even high degree of probability, and furthermore, even if all its claims be admitted, would lead to a result far short of theism--a mere indefinite first cause, an Architect of the universe, etc. Each one, however, adds its quota to a great ***cumulative*** argument, which, taken in its entirety, raises an exceedingly high presumption, which amounts to "***moral***" though possibly not intellectual proof. And, after all, "probability is the guide of ***life***."

And this is all that the Fathers, or Christian apologists, generally, would claim for the theistic argument. It is a ***practical***, not a theoretical proof, and it is in this way that the early Christian writers seem to regard it. They resort to it most frequently to show that the Christian doctrine of God is not contrary to reason nor inconsistent with the nature of things, and to demonstrate that such a conception is demanded by man's very nature. In a word, their use of the argument is confirmatory and explanatory rather than by way of absolute proof and demonstration.

This attitude towards and use of the theistic argument, so radically different from that of the Greek philosophers, perpetuated itself in the post-Nicene literature of the Christian Church, and, in its main features, remained unaltered, until the time when men who had abandoned the faith in the Word which had been the main stay of the ante-Nicene writers, and who yet were unwilling to abandon the great theistic idea for which the world was indebted to Christianity alone, sought to justify this idea on the basis of reason. It took the scepticism of a Hume and the criticism of a Kant, and the re-adjustment of all their followers to bring us back at the close of this nineteenth century into substantial agreement with the common-sense estimate placed upon the theistic argument by the ante-Nicene Fathers.

NOTES:

[92] *History of Philosophy*, Vol. I, Sec. 4.

[93] Burnet: *Early Greek Philosophy*, p. 25.

[94] *Stromata*, II, iv.

VITA.

The writer was born April 24, 1869, in Ann Arbor, Michigan. He attended the Ann Arbor Public Schools and the Ann Arbor High School. In 1892 he received the degree of A. B. from the University of Michigan. In 1895 he graduated from the General Theological Seminary, New York, and was awarded the degree of B. D., which was formally conferred in accordance with the rules of the Seminary one year later. In 1896, he received the degree of A. M. from the University of Michigan. He pursued studies in Philosophy at Harvard University during the first term of the year 1896-7, and at Columbia University from February, 1897, to February, 1898. He has been the post-graduate scholar of the Church University Board of Regents from July, 1895, to the present time.

www.bookjungle.com *email: sales@bookjungle.com fax: 630-214-0564 mail: Book Jungle PO Box 2226 Champaign, IL 61825*

The Codes Of Hammurabi And Moses
W. W. Davies

QTY

The discovery of the Hammurabi Code is one of the greatest achievements of archaeology, and is of paramount interest, not only to the student of the Bible, but also to all those interested in ancient history...

Religion   **ISBN:** *1-59462-338-4*   **Pages:**132
MSRP $12.95

The Theory of Moral Sentiments
Adam Smith

QTY

This work from 1749. contains original theories of conscience amd moral judgment and it is the foundation for systemof morals.

Philosophy   **ISBN:** *1-59462-777-0*   **Pages:**536
MSRP $19.95

Jessica's First Prayer
Hesba Stretton

QTY

In a screened and secluded corner of one of the many railway-bridges which span the streets of London there could be seen a few years ago, from five o'clock every morning until half past eight, a tidily set-out coffee-stall, consisting of a trestle and board, upon which stood two large tin cans, with a small fire of charcoal burning under each so as to keep the coffee boiling during the early hours of the morning when the work-people were thronging into the city on their way to their daily toil...

Childrens   **ISBN:** *1-59462-373-2*   **Pages:**84
MSRP $9.95

My Life and Work
Henry Ford

QTY

Henry Ford revolutionized the world with his implementation of mass production for the Model T automobile. Gain valuable business insight into his life and work with his own auto-biography... "We have only started on our development of our country we have not as yet, with all our talk of wonderful progress, done more than scratch the surface. The progress has been wonderful enough but..."

Biographies/   **ISBN:** *1-59462-198-5*   **Pages:**300
MSRP $21.95

www.bookjungle.com *email: sales@bookjungle.com fax: 630-214-0564 mail: Book Jungle PO Box 2226 Champaign, IL 61825*

The Art of Cross-Examination
Francis Wellman

QTY

I presume it is the experience of every author, after his first book is published upon an important subject, to be almost overwhelmed with a wealth of ideas and illustrations which could readily have been included in his book, and which to his own mind, at least, seem to make a second edition inevitable. Such certainly was the case with me; and when the first edition had reached its sixth impression in five months, I rejoiced to learn that it seemed to my publishers that the book had met with a sufficiently favorable reception to justify a second and considerably enlarged edition. ...

Reference   ISBN: *1-59462-647-2*

Pages:412
MSRP *$19.95*

On the Duty of Civil Disobedience
Henry David Thoreau

QTY

Thoreau wrote his famous essay, On the Duty of Civil Disobedience, as a protest against an unjust but popular war and the immoral but popular institution of slave-owning. He did more than write—he declined to pay his taxes, and was hauled off to gaol in consequence. Who can say how much this refusal of his hastened the end of the war and of slavery ?

Law   ISBN: *1-59462-747-9*

Pages:48
MSRP *$7.45*

Dream Psychology Psychoanalysis for Beginners
Sigmund Freud

QTY

Sigmund Freud, born Sigismund Schlomo Freud (May 6, 1856 - September 23, 1939), was a Jewish-Austrian neurologist and psychiatrist who co-founded the psychoanalytic school of psychology. Freud is best known for his theories of the unconscious mind, especially involving the mechanism of repression; his redefinition of sexual desire as mobile and directed towards a wide variety of objects; and his therapeutic techniques, especially his understanding of transference in the therapeutic relationship and the presumed value of dreams as sources of insight into unconscious desires.

Psychology   ISBN: *1-59462-905-6*

Pages:196
MSRP *$15.45*

The Miracle of Right Thought
Orison Swett Marden

QTY

Believe with all of your heart that you will do what you were made to do. When the mind has once formed the habit of holding cheerful, happy, prosperous pictures, it will not be easy to form the opposite habit. It does not matter how improbable or how far away this realization may see, or how dark the prospects may be, if we visualize them as best we can, as vividly as possible, hold tenaciously to them and vigorously struggle to attain them, they will gradually become actualized, realized in the life. But a desire, a longing without endeavor, a yearning abandoned or held indifferently will vanish without realization.

Self Help   ISBN: *1-59462-644-8*

Pages:360
MSRP *$25.45*

www.bookjungle.com email: sales@bookjungle.com fax: 630-214-0564 mail: Book Jungle PO Box 2226 Champaign, IL 61825

QTY

- [ ] **The Rosicrucian Cosmo-Conception Mystic Christianity** *by Max Heindel* ISBN: *1-59462-188-8* **$38.95**
  The Rosicrucian Cosmo-conception is not dogmatic, neither does it appeal to any other authority than the reason of the student. It is: not controversial, but is: sent forth in the, hope that it may help to clear... *New Age/Religion Pages 646*

- [ ] **Abandonment To Divine Providence** *by Jean-Pierre de Caussade* ISBN: *1-59462-228-0* **$25.95**
  "The Rev. Jean Pierre de Caussade was one of the most remarkable spiritual writers of the Society of Jesus in France in the 18th Century. His death took place at Toulouse in 1751. His works have gone through many editions and have been republished... *Inspirational/Religion Pages 400*

- [ ] **Mental Chemistry** *by Charles Haanel* ISBN: *1-59462-192-6* **$23.95**
  Mental Chemistry allows the change of material conditions by combining and appropriately utilizing the power of the mind. Much like applied chemistry creates something new and unique out of careful combinations of chemicals the mastery of mental chemistry... *New Age Pages 354*

- [ ] **The Letters of Robert Browning and Elizabeth Barret Barrett 1845-1846 vol II** ISBN: *1-59462-193-4* **$35.95**
  by Robert Browning and Elizabeth Barrett *Biographies Pages 596*

- [ ] **Gleanings In Genesis (volume I)** *by Arthur W. Pink* ISBN: *1-59462-130-6* **$27.45**
  Appropriately has Genesis been termed "the seed plot of the Bible" for in it we have, in germ form, almost all of the great doctrines which are afterwards fully developed in the books of Scripture which follow... *Religion/Inspirational Pages 420*

- [ ] **The Master Key** *by L. W. de Laurence* ISBN: *1-59462-001-6* **$30.95**
  In no branch of human knowledge has there been a more lively increase of the spirit of research during the past few years than in the study of Psychology, Concentration and Mental Discipline. The requests for authentic lessons in Thought Control, Mental Discipline and... *New Age/Business Pages 422*

- [ ] **The Lesser Key Of Solomon Goetia** *by L. W. de Laurence* ISBN: *1-59462-092-X* **$9.95**
  This translation of the first book of the "Lernegton" which is now for the first time made accessible to students of Talismanic Magic was done, after careful collation and edition, from numerous Ancient Manuscripts in Hebrew, Latin, and French... *New Age/Occult Pages 92*

- [ ] **Rubaiyat Of Omar Khayyam** *by Edward Fitzgerald* ISBN:*1-59462-332-5* **$13.95**
  Edward Fitzgerald, whom the world has already learned, in spite of his own efforts to remain within the shadow of anonymity, to look upon as one of the rarest poets of the century, was born at Bredfield, in Suffolk, on the 31st of March, 1809. He was the third son of John Purcell... *Music Pages 172*

- [ ] **Ancient Law** *by Henry Maine* ISBN: *1-59462-128-4* **$29.95**
  The chief object of the following pages is to indicate some of the earliest ideas of mankind, as they are reflected in Ancient Law, and to point out the relation of those ideas to modern thought. *Religion/History Pages 452*

- [ ] **Far-Away Stories** *by William J. Locke* ISBN: *1-59462-129-2* **$19.45**
  "Good wine needs no bush, but a collection of mixed vintages does. And this book is just such a collection. Some of the stories I do not want to remain buried for ever in the museum files of dead magazine-numbers an author's not unpardonable vanity..." *Fiction Pages 272*

- [ ] **Life of David Crockett** *by David Crockett* ISBN: *1-59462-250-7* **$27.45**
  "Colonel David Crockett was one of the most remarkable men of the times in which he lived. Born in humble life, but gifted with a strong will, an indomitable courage, and unremitting perseverance... *Biographies/New Age Pages 424*

- [ ] **Lip-Reading** *by Edward Nitchie* ISBN: *1-59462-206-X* **$25.95**
  Edward B. Nitchie, founder of the New York School for the Hard of Hearing, now the Nitchie School of Lip-Reading, Inc, wrote "LIP-READING Principles and Practice". The development and perfecting of this meritorious work on lip-reading was an undertaking... *How-to Pages 400*

- [ ] **A Handbook of Suggestive Therapeutics, Applied Hypnotism, Psychic Science** ISBN: *1-59462-214-0* **$24.95**
  by Henry Munro *Health/New Age/Health/Self-help Pages 376*

- [ ] **A Doll's House: and Two Other Plays** *by Henrik Ibsen* ISBN: *1-59462-112-8* **$19.95**
  Henrik Ibsen created this classic when in revolutionary 1848 Rome. Introducing some striking concepts in playwriting for the realist genre, this play has been studied the world over. *Fiction/Classics/Plays 308*

- [ ] **The Light of Asia** *by sir Edwin Arnold* ISBN: *1-59462-204-3* **$13.95**
  In this poetic masterpiece, Edwin Arnold describes the life and teachings of Buddha. The man who was to become known as Buddha to the world was born as Prince Gautama of India but he rejected the worldly riches and abandoned the reigns of power when... *Religion/History/Biographies Pages 170*

- [ ] **The Complete Works of Guy de Maupassant** *by Guy de Maupassant* ISBN: *1-59462-157-8* **$16.95**
  "For days and days, nights and nights, I had dreamed of that first kiss which was to consecrate our engagement, and I knew not on what spot I should put my lips..." *Fiction/Classics Pages 240*

- [ ] **The Art of Cross-Examination** *by Francis L. Wellman* ISBN: *1-59462-309-0* **$26.95**
  Written by a renowned trial lawyer, Wellman imparts his experience and uses case studies to explain how to use psychology to extract desired information through questioning. *How-to/Science/Reference Pages 408*

- [ ] **Answered or Unanswered?** *by Louisa Vaughan* ISBN: *1-59462-248-5* **$10.95**
  Miracles of Faith in China *Religion Pages 112*

- [ ] **The Edinburgh Lectures on Mental Science (1909)** *by Thomas* ISBN: *1-59462-008-3* **$11.95**
  This book contains the substance of a course of lectures recently given by the writer in the Queen Street Hall, Edinburgh. Its purpose is to indicate the Natural Principles governing the relation between Mental Action and Material Conditions... *New Age/Psychology Pages 148*

- [ ] **Ayesha** *by H. Rider Haggard* ISBN: *1-59462-301-5* **$24.95**
  Verily and indeed it is the unexpected that happens! Probably if there was one person upon the earth from whom the Editor of this, and of a certain previous history, did not expect to hear again... *Classics Pages 380*

- [ ] **Ayala's Angel** *by Anthony Trollope* ISBN: *1-59462-352-X* **$29.95**
  The two girls were both pretty, but Lucy who was twenty-one who supposed to be simple and comparatively unattractive, whereas Ayala was credited, as her Bombwhat romantic name might show, with poetic charm and a taste for romance. Ayala when her father died was nineteen... *Fiction Pages 484*

- [ ] **The American Commonwealth** *by James Bryce* ISBN: *1-59462-286-8* **$34.45**
  An interpretation of American democratic political theory. It examines political mechanics and society from the perspective of Scotsman James Bryce *Politics Pages 572*

- [ ] **Stories of the Pilgrims** *by Margaret P. Pumphrey* ISBN: *1-59462-116-0* **$17.95**
  This book explores pilgrims religious oppression in England as well as their escape to Holland and eventual crossing to America on the Mayflower, and their early days in New England... *History Pages 268*

www.bookjungle.com *email: sales@bookjungle.com fax: 630-214-0564 mail: Book Jungle PO Box 2226 Champaign, IL 61825*

			QTY
The Fasting Cure *by Sinclair Upton*	ISBN: *1-59462-222-1*	**$13.95**	☐
In the Cosmopolitan Magazine for May, 1910, and in the Contemporary Review (London) for April, 1910, I published an article dealing with my experiences in fasting. I have written a great many magazine articles, but never one which attracted so much attention...		*New Age/Self Help/Health Pages 164*	
Hebrew Astrology *by Sepharial*	ISBN: *1-59462-308-2*	**$13.45**	☐
In these days of advanced thinking it is a matter of common observation that we have left many of the old landmarks behind and that we are now pressing forward to greater heights and to a wider horizon than that which represented the mind-content of our progenitors...		*Astrology Pages 144*	
Thought Vibration or The Law of Attraction in the Thought World	ISBN: *1-59462-127-6*	**$12.95**	☐
by William Walker Atkinson		*Psychology/Religion Pages 144*	
Optimism *by Helen Keller*	ISBN: *1-59462-108-X*	**$15.95**	☐
Helen Keller was blind, deaf, and mute since 19 months old, yet famously learned how to overcome these handicaps, communicate with the world, and spread her lectures promoting optimism. An inspiring read for everyone...		*Biographies/Inspirational Pages 84*	
Sara Crewe *by Frances Burnett*	ISBN: *1-59462-360-0*	**$9.45**	☐
In the first place, Miss Minchin lived in London. Her home was a large, dull, tall one, in a large, dull square, where all the houses were alike, and all the sparrows were alike, and where all the door-knockers made the same heavy sound...		*Childrens/Classic Pages 88*	
The Autobiography of Benjamin Franklin *by Benjamin Franklin*	ISBN: *1-59462-135-7*	**$24.95**	☐
The Autobiography of Benjamin Franklin has probably been more extensively read than any other American historical work, and no other book of its kind has had such ups and downs of fortune. Franklin lived for many years in England, where he was agent...		*Biographies/History Pages 332*	

Name	
Email	
Telephone	
Address	
City, State ZIP	

☐ Credit Card   ☐ Check / Money Order

Credit Card Number	
Expiration Date	
Signature	

Please Mail to: Book Jungle
PO Box 2226
Champaign, IL 61825
or Fax to: 630-214-0564

ORDERING INFORMATION
web: www.bookjungle.com
email: sales@bookjungle.com
fax: 630-214-0564
mail: Book Jungle PO Box 2226 Champaign, IL 61825
or PayPal *to sales@bookjungle.com*

Please contact us for bulk discounts

DIRECT-ORDER TERMS

20% Discount if You Order Two or More Books
Free Domestic Shipping!
Accepted: Master Card, Visa, Discover, American Express

www.ingramcontent.com/pod-product-compliance
Lightning Source LLC
Chambersburg PA
CBHW081330040426
42453CB00013B/2364